BUILDING
a NEW NATION:
the FEDERALIST ERA

1789–1801

BUILDING
a NEW NATION:
the FEDERALIST ERA

1789–1801

Christopher Collier
James Lincoln Collier

BENCHMARK BOOKS

MARSHALL CAVENDISH
NEW YORK

ACKNOWLEDGMENT: The authors wish to thank Stanley M. Elkins, Sidham Clark Parsons Professor Emeritus of History, Smith College, for his careful reading of the text of this volume of The Drama of American History and his thoughtful and useful comments. This work has been much improved by Professor Elkins's notes. The authors are deeply in his debt but, of course, assume full responsibility for the substance of the work, including any errors that may appear.

Photo research by James Lincoln Collier.

COVER PHOTO: Abby Aldrich Rockafeller Folk Art Center, Williamsburg

PICTURE CREDITS: The photographs in this book are used by permission and through the courtesy of:
Corbis-Bettman: 16, 18, 20, 22, 24, 26 (top), 26 (bottom), 31, 32, 33, 36, 38, 40, 46 (top), 46 (bottom), 52, 56, 57, 59, 63, 65, 69, 73, 74, 81, 82, 84. *Independence National Historic Park*: 10, 13, 43, 49, 51, 53, 62, 66 (left), 66 (right), 75, 78. *Colonial Williamsburg Foundation*: 37, 50.
Abby Aldrich Rockafeller Folk Art Center, Williamsburg: 12.

Benchmark Books
Marshall Cavendish Corporation
99 White Plains Road
Tarrytown, New York 10591-9001

©1999 Christopher Collier and James Lincoln Collier

Library of Congress Cataloging-in-Publication Data

Collier, Christopher, date
Building a new nation, 1789–1801 / Christopher Collier and James Lincoln Collier
p. cm. — (The drama of American history)
Includes bibliographical references and index.
Summary: Examines the events and personalities involved in the political development of the United States in the period following the creation of the Constitution.
ISBN 0-7614-0776-6
1. United States—Politics and government—1789–1809—Juvenile literature.
[1. United States—History—Constitutional period, 1789–1809.] I. Collier, James Lincoln, date.
II. Title. III. Series: Collier, Christopher, date. Drama of American history.
E310.C67 1999   97-26491
973.4—dc21   CIP
                                AC

Printed in Italy

1 3 5 6 4 2

CONTENTS

PREFACE

Over many years of both teaching and writing for students at all levels, from grammar school to graduate school, it has been borne in on us that many, if not most, American history textbooks suffer from trying to include everything of any moment in the history of the nation. Students become lost in a swamp of factual information, and as a consequence lose track of how those facts fit together and why they are significant and relevant to the world today.

In this series, our effort has been to strip the vast amount of available detail down to a central core. Our aim is to draw in bold strokes, providing enough information, but no more than is necessary, to bring out the basic themes of the American story, and what they mean to us now. We believe that it is surely more important for students to grasp the underlying concepts and ideas that emerge from the movement of history, than to memorize an array of facts and figures.

The difference between this series and many standard texts lies in what has been left out. We are convinced that students will better remember the important themes if they are not buried under a heap of names, dates, and places.

In this sense, our primary goal is what might be called citizenship education. We think it is critically important for America as a nation and Americans as individuals to understand the origins and workings of the public institutions that are central to American society. We have asked ourselves again and again what is most important for citizens of our democracy to know so they can most effectively make the system work for them and the nation. For this reason, we have focused on political and institutional history, leaving social and cultural history less well developed.

This series is divided into volumes that move chronologically through the American story. Each is built around a single topic, such as the Pilgrims, the Constitutional Convention, or immigration. Each volume has been written so that it can stand alone, for students who wish to research a given topic. As a consequence, in many cases material from previous volumes is repeated, usually in abbreviated form, to set the topic in its historical context. That is to say, students of the Constitutional Convention must be given some idea of relations with England, and why the Revolution was fought, even though the material was covered in detail in a previous volume. Readers should find that each volume tells an entire story that can be read with or without reference to other volumes.

Despite our belief that it is of the first importance to outline sharply basic concepts and generalizations, we have not neglected the great dramas of American history. The stories that will hold the attention of students are here, and we believe they will help the concepts they illustrate to stick in their minds. We think, for example, that knowing of Abraham Baldwin's brave and dramatic decision to vote with the small states at the Constitutional Convention will bring alive the Connecticut Compromise, out of which grew the American Senate.

Each of these volumes has been read by esteemed specialists in its particular topic; we have benefited from their comments.

CHAPTER I

Setting Up a New House

W hen an architect draws up a plan for a house, he has a pretty good idea of what the house will be like. He knows how it will look from the outside, where people will hang their coats when they come in, whether the sun will shine on the breakfast table. Indeed, with modern computer equipment, he can actually make pictures of the rooms to show to his clients.

This is not so with a plan for a government. An architect can predict how a house will look because it is made with materials he knows all about. A democratic government is made up of people, chosen by other people, to act upon people—of the people, for the people, by the people, as the famous saying goes. And people are not nearly as predictable as wood and stone.

The Constitution of the United States, which those brilliant and politically experienced men had drawn up in Philadelphia during that long hot summer of 1787, was a *plan* for a government. It described how the Congress would be elected, what duties the president would have, what authority would be left to the states, and much else. (Readers interested in the creation of the American Constitution can consult *Creating the*

In this building, now called Independence Hall, some of America's most brilliant leaders met in the summer of 1787 to write the Constitution. In so doing, they laid out the plan for the U.S. government. Two years later, George Washington, his cabinet, and the Congress had to apply the document in practice.

Constitution, the sixth book in this series.) The big questions were: Would the plan work? And if it did work, how would it work?

For example, would Congress and the president be forever squabbling over their powers, so that in the end nothing got done? Would Congressmen begin to quarrel among themselves, with representatives of western farmers, city merchants, southern planters, northern shippers, all trying to get the most for themselves and in the end paralyzing government? Would the Senate block actions of the House? Again, the Constitution was not entirely clear about what the Supreme Court could and couldn't do. Americans had designed a government, but would they be able to put into practice what they had agreed to in theory? That would be the real test.

The story of what historians call the Federal Era, the period of the first twelve years of the new United States, is not so dramatic as the fighting of the Revolution or the writing of the Constitution. It is nonetheless one of the most critical periods that the nation has ever faced, for in this time the brand-new government put the Constitution into practice. In so doing, it established a lot of the basic ways of doing things that the government follows today.

The United States in 1788 was considerably different from what it is today. Most Americans—about 90 percent—were farmers of one kind or another. The majority of them lived on independent family farms, where husbands, wives, sons, and daughters worked together to grow and make most of what they needed. They raised cattle, hogs, chickens, sheep; grew wheat, corn, and many other crops. They spun wool and cotton to make yarn, wove the yarn into cloth, sewed the cloth into shirts and skirts. They sold their extra wheat, beef, and pork to traders in exchange for a little money with which to pay their taxes and buy the few things, like axes and needles, that they couldn't make for themselves. Sometimes they did without money altogether and bartered with storekeepers for these things.

Not everybody lived this way. In the big cities like New York, Philadelphia, Charleston, and Boston, merchants lived by shipping out American wheat, beef, corn, tobacco, pork, and importing European tables, glassware, farm implements. In New England especially there were shipbuilders, sailors, fishermen, who got their livelihoods from the sea. A small but growing number of manufacturers ran little factories to

Here is the home of a prosperous farmer, David Turning, showing livestock, barns, and a servant or slave plowing a field. The Turning family is in the right foreground. The picture, painted by Edward Hicks in the 1840s, was as the artist remembered the farm to be in 1787. Many farmers were not this well outfitted. Especially on the frontier, farmhouses might be little more than cabins. Generally speaking, though, farmers were doing well.

smelt iron ore, and make guns, axes, glasses, dishes. But most people lived off the land.

A great many of these Americans had been opposed to the Constitution when it was presented to them and voted against it. But surprisingly, once it was ratified, even those most strongly opposed quickly came to accept it. Now, most Americans were looking to the new government to solve a great many problems the country was facing. What were the problems?

For one, after losing the Revolution, the British had shut Americans out of ports in England and in its colonies elsewhere, especially the West Indies, ending a trade that had for over a century been at the heart of American commerce. For another, the British, contrary to the peace treaty, still kept troops in the Great Lakes area, who, so Americans thought, were encouraging Indians to attack American farmers in the western lands across the Allegheny Mountains. The Spanish claimed the

A view of Second Street in Philadelphia, about 1800. Although some manufacturing existed in cities, most businesses of the day were in commerce—they bought and sold goods, and they shipped large quantities of farmers' produce to other parts of the United States, the West Indies, Europe, and even China.

Mississippi and the vast territory to the west of it. They had corked up the river with the settlement at New Orleans, which meant that Americans could ship goods out of the western areas only with the permission of the Spanish. And on top of everything, the United States owed huge sums of money it had borrowed to fight the Revolution.

Not every American was worried about all of these problems, but most Americans were worried about some of them. Merchants, shippers, and farmers who had formerly sold pork, corn, tobacco, and other goods to London or the West Indies wanted some kind of treaty with England that would open up that trade again. Farmers at the edge of the wilderness, in places like upstate New York, western Pennsylvania, and what is now Ohio, wanted the British out of the Great Lakes forts and protection from the Indians. Wealthy men who had lent money to the government, and soldiers who had taken IOUs for their army service, wanted government debts paid. These were practical problems, and it remained to be seen if the government created by the Constitution would be able to solve them.

CHAPTER II

The First Elections

The first thing that had to be done in 1788 under the new Constitution was to elect a government. We need to understand that, at that time, there were in the United States no such things as political parties. Nor did Americans want any. They had witnessed the operation of political parties in England during the years leading up to the Revolution, and they had not liked what they saw. Political parties were always quarreling, and they always, it seemed, were more interested in beating out each other than in doing what was best for their country. Furthermore, they were corrupt: Party members bribed each other, gave their friends easy, well-paying jobs in government, even when they were incompetent. Parties, as Americans saw them, were worse than useless, and throughout the Federal Era many of the most important Americans spoke out against them. George Washington himself devoted a good portion of his famous Farewell Address to the bad effects of political parties. He told Americans, "Let me now . . . warn you in the most solemn manner against the baneful effects of the spirit of party," and said that parties were the people's "worst enemy." Parties, he believed, created friction and antagonisms that worked

A newspaper drawing of scenes from the Republican National Convention of 1884. Founding Fathers like Washington and Madison would have hated such noisy, festive nominating conventions and the party system they grew out of. Historians believe, however, that the party system was an inevitable, even essential, outgrowth of democratic government.

against people trying to find good solutions to their common problems.

But how do you conduct elections without political parties to put up nominees? So far as the presidency was concerned, according to the new Constitution, the choice would be made by electors from each state, chosen by whatever system each state set up. In the majority of states, the legislature chose the electors, but in other states the people chose more directly through various systems. In any case, in this first election, it did not much matter. Everybody knew that George Washington must be president, and he was elected unanimously. His vice president was a Massachusetts man, John Adams, who had been prominent in the revolt against England. Adams was chosen in part to balance the southerner Washington with a northerner.

The first members of the new Congress were also chosen as the Constitution directed. Two senators were chosen from each state by the state legislatures. Representatives were chosen from each state directly by the voters. Not surprisingly, most of the new Congressmen were people who generally agreed with George Washington on most important issues. He would have a Congress he could get along with. Washington was going to set both the policies and the tone of the new government and we must therefore know something about who he was and what he thought.

Historians today are trying to get away from the "great man" theory of history, which emphasizes the deeds of kings, generals, presidents, and rebel leaders. Instead, they tend to focus on the feelings and doings of ordinary people. Most historians, however, agree that Washington was one of those rare beings, a truly great man who shaped the course of events around him. Without Washington the United States today might be quite different; indeed, the experiment might have failed, and the union fallen apart.

George Washington was not an original thinker—not an intellectual genius like such of his associates as Alexander Hamilton or Thomas Jefferson, not a clever inventor and diplomat like Benjamin Franklin, not a fiery speech maker like Patrick Henry or a sophisticated constitutional theorist like James Madison. Washington's strength was his character. Absolutely fearless in battle, he would rush into the line of fire to encourage his men, later to find bullet holes in his hat. He was one of the best athletes of his era, a rangy six footer, a skillful rider, who again and again trekked through hundreds of miles of wilderness on his missions. He was judicious, carefully weighing the evidence on all sides of every question, rarely allowing himself to be swayed by feelings, except his own desire to do the right thing. Historians are amazed by how seldom he made a misjudgment on an important matter.

George Washington was revered by Americans of his day, was unanimously elected president twice, and could have gone on being elected if he had wished. This homespun drawing of Washington and his wife, Martha, was typical of thousands of images of the first president that were hung on walls in American homes.

George Washington had his weaknesses, of course. He had a quick temper and would occasionally blow up and shout at his assistants. He, as much as anybody, liked to sit around over dinner drinking wine and telling stories with his friends. He liked cards, he liked hunting, he liked buying fancy clothes. But the key to his character was his determination to cure himself of weaknesses and always do what was right. Perhaps more than any other American in a high place, he succeeded.

George Washington believed in strong government. He had spent desperate years trying to fight the Revolution against the British under a government that often failed to give him the men and materiel he needed. He had worked to get a strong central government written into the Constitution. It is important for us to understand this, for the new government under President Washington was about to set the direction for the nation for years to come.

Inevitably, Washington chose for his assistants in the new government people who thought the way he did. One of the most important of these people was Alexander Hamilton. A favorite of Washington, Hamilton had as a young man served on Washington's staff during the Revolution and had fought bravely in battle. He was also one of the most brilliant men at the Constitutional Convention of 1787.

Alexander Hamilton was born on the island of Nevis in the West Indies. His mother was poor, and his father a ne'er-do-well son of Scottish nobility who in any case had left the family early. Hamilton had to make his way himself. Fortunately he was personable, handsome, though short and delicate looking, and very smart. He was taken up by a local merchant and by the age of fourteen was running the store. Other supporters sent him to New York to be educated. Still a teenager as the Revolution was coming on, he wrote a series of widely read pamphlets on the conflict. Washington met him and quickly made him an aide. Hamilton became a colonel when just out of his teens. In 1780, as the Revolution was winding down, he married into a wealthy and well-connected New York family. His political future was assured.

For all of his brilliance, however, Hamilton was a rash and imperious man who tended to get himself into quarrels; in fact, he died in a duel that he could have avoided, but which he felt honor bound to fight.

When Washington became president in 1789, he made Hamilton his secretary of the treasury. Today this post is seen as less important than secretary of state or of defense. Hamilton felt otherwise. In England, at the time, the head of finance was almost equivalent to the prime minister. Hamilton believed that the official who controlled the money controlled all, and he assumed that he was Washington's right-hand man—indeed, that he was the real power behind the throne. He was determined that the new government should do what he thought it ought to do.

For his secretary of state, Washington chose a brilliant Virginian, the principal author of the Declaration of Independence, Thomas Jefferson, whose ideas, as we shall soon see, did not always agree with those of the imperious Hamilton. Washington chose another Virginian he knew well, Edmund Randolph, as his attorney general.

The new government was much smaller than the one we have today. There were no such officers as secretary of labor, secretary of commerce, and the like. Nonetheless, in Hamilton, Jefferson, and Randolph, along with Vice President John Adams, Washington had created the beginnings of the cabinet system so important to us today. Here is an excellent example of how the new government was fleshing out the plan laid down by the Constitution. The Constitution says nothing about a

Edmund Randolph, America's first attorney general, was a good politician but a cautious man who would not rush into trouble. With Jefferson, Hamilton and Vice President Adams, he was part of the first presidential cabinet, Washington's establishment of which set a precedent that has been followed ever since.

cabinet. It merely alludes to "the principal officer in each of the executive departments." Particular officers such as the attorney general or secretary of state are not mentioned. These officers were established by Congress. The Constitution says only that the president, with the advice and consent of the Senate, could appoint the necessary officers.

Washington did not merely appoint such officers but sought their advice, either in writing or in conversation, and occasionally as a group where they would discuss problems confronting the government. In so doing, he created the institution of the cabinet which today still meets regularly with the president to give him advice. The Constitution did not establish a cabinet; but it did not prohibit one either. Washington saw the value of such a body and put it in motion. These first governmental officers, thus, were setting the country off on paths of their own choosing. And many of the decisions they made continue to affect us today.

The most important of these men at the outset proved to be the secretary of the treasury, Alexander Hamilton. He firmly believed that developing a sound, profitable commerce would be critical to the success of the new country. It was not enough for this country of farmers merely to produce enough for themselves and rest content: It must develop an international trade not only in foodstuffs but in manufactured goods, despite the fact that American industry was still very small potatoes compared to that in Europe, where the industrial revolution was throwing up factories everywhere. Here we can see Hamilton's competitive streak coming out: At the time, the United States was an unimportant country in a backwater. Hamilton wanted his country to be a great nation, as powerful and feared as any of the European nations, especially England and France.

From this, certain ideas followed. For one, it was absolutely crucial that the new government establish its credit everywhere with nations and with their merchants—businessmen, to use the modern word. In the late eighteenth century, the complex system of intermeshed banks through which business is done today did not exist: You could not simply send somebody a check that he could cash at a distant bank. Furthermore, it was inconvenient, not to say risky, to send trunks of cash in the form of gold and silver coins long distances. Instead, merchants did business on credit, "charging," as we say today, what they bought, and later on balancing the accounts. Debts were actually traded almost like money. If merchant Sayles owed money to glassmaker Dubois in France but in turn was owed money by tobacco broker Pipes in England, he might "pay" Dubois with Pipes's debt to him. The whole system could work with money changing hands only infrequently. But it meant that everybody had to trust everybody else—everyone's *credit* had to be good.

The problem was that the credit of the new United States wasn't much good. The Revolution had been fought on borrowed money, and

In the early days, the United States did not have official paper money. Business was done with coins, like these gold doubloons struck in 1787 in New York. While coins were convenient for day-to-day business, they were difficult to use for large-scale commerce. Merchants usually traded through an international network of credit, with actual money changing hands infrequently. Hamilton wanted to make sure the credit of the new United States was solid.

now, six years after the peace treaty had been signed, the debts had not been paid. The national government owed $42 million to Americans and others around the world, and the states owed another $21 million—huge sums for that day.

Hamilton worked out a daring plan. The U.S. government would be responsible for all the debts, state as well as federal. The government would pay interest on the debt out of the money it collected through duties on imports, excise taxes on whiskey and certain other goods, and the sale of the western lands. There were a lot of objections to this plan. Among others, some states, like Virginia, had already paid off most of their war debts, and Virginians did not see why they ought to be taxed to pay off the war debts of other states.

But there was more to Hamilton's plan than this. Hamilton believed that America needed industry—factories spinning thread, weaving cloth, smelting iron, casting axe heads, forming glassware and dishes, and much else. Such factories existed, but they were small and few, and Americans still had to buy most of their manufactured goods from Europe. Why should Americans spend money in England and France for goods that they might be able to make at home? Hamilton asked.

But industry could not be built without capital. Somebody had to put up the money for the buildings, tools, and equipment to get started with. Hamilton reasoned that, to create this capital, he must see to it that large sums of money accumulated in the hands of people who would use it to start up new businesses. He planned to do this by "funding" the huge debt. That is to say, he would not pay off the debt. Instead he would issue government bonds and exchange them for the IOUs of the old government. These bonds would pay interest to their owners, who would mostly be wealthy people who could use the income from the bonds to invest in new businesses. To put it bluntly, Hamilton wanted to make the rich richer so they could build up capital that they would invest for the good of the nation as a whole.

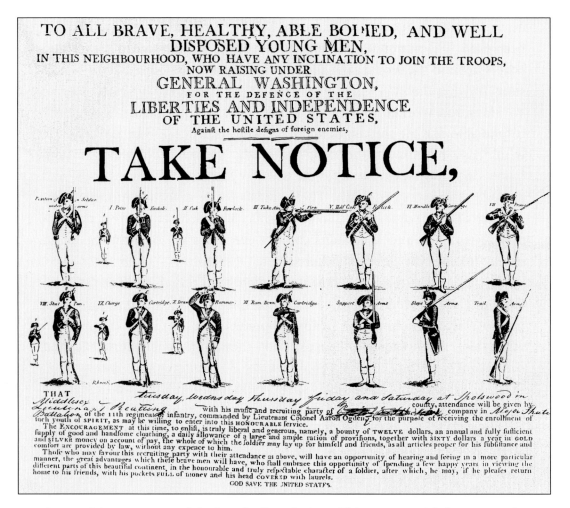

A recruiting poster used during the Revolution. This poster said that a recruit would have the "opportunity of . . . spending a few happy years in viewing the different parts of this beautiful continent . . . [and] return home to his friends, with his pockets FULL of money." Few soldiers, of course, were very happy in the war, and many never returned to their friends. Moreover, most were paid in government IOUs instead of pocketfuls of money. Later, many had to sell their IOUs, at a fraction of their value, to speculators. It seemed unfair to many that the speculators, rather than the soldiers, could cash in on Hamilton's plan for funding the debt.

There was a second part to Hamilton's plan. He knew that most Americans were more attached to their states than to the United States. On the other hand, he believed that merchants were more likely to "think nationally," because they were often dealing with buyers and sellers in distant states, or even in foreign countries.

But, still, many Americans owned IOUs issued by state governments. The new Constitution had taken from the states the power to collect duties on imports and exports. They would have a hard time paying their debts. Hamilton persuaded Congress to assume—that is, to adopt—the state debts and pay them off. This meant that people who were owed money by the states might shift their primary loyalty to the United States. Thus another group of wealthy people—who would get richer and have money to invest in factories—would also give their support to the new federal government.

Hamilton's idea of funding the state and national debt was very controversial. One serious problem with it was that a lot of the bonds would go to the people who had not originally lent money to the government but had bought the IOUs of other people at low prices. For example, during the Revolution, many soldiers took IOUs instead of money from the government, which had none to pay them with. When these soldiers went back to their farms, they often found themselves desperate for hard cash—the gold and silver coins that everybody at the time believed was "real money." They therefore might sell to a speculator a government IOU worth a hundred dollars, for just a few dollars. Many people believed that these speculators ought not to make windfall profits from these IOUs; instead, the money should go to the soldiers and others who had originally been given them.

A second idea Hamilton had, related to the first, was to create a national bank—the Bank of the United States. The government would use this bank as a place to deposit its money and to pay its bills. More important, this bank would make loans to private citizens—for invest-

At left, one of the thousands of water mills dotting the United States in the early years and supplying most of the power for the nation's infant industry. Below, a drawing of a factory for making steam engines in Birmingham, England. At the time, the English were far ahead of the rest of the world in advancing the industrial revolution.

ment, Hamilton hoped. These loan "notes" promised that the government would trade them in for hard cash. These notes could be passed from hand to hand, and would become, in effect, paper money, like the five- and ten- and twenty-dollar bills we use for money today. Paper money would greatly aid in the development of commerce. Though the bank would be backed by the U.S. government and be able to make a profit on lending public money, it was to be controlled by private individuals elected by stockholders. Hamilton believed that the way to get the most efficiency was to give the owners and managers a personal stake in the success of the business.

Finally, Hamilton proposed a system of bonuses and other incentives for people who would invent new and better ways of manufacturing things.

Behind all of these financial schemes of Hamilton was his deep concern to hold the United States together and build it into a mighty nation. There was an element of pride, even overwhelming pride, in this vision. Not only Hamilton, but Washington and many of those around them, wanted to gain for themselves eternal fame as founders of a great nation, in the same way that the heroes of the ancient Roman Empire, about whom they had all read a great deal, had found eternal fame. Hamilton and many of the others believed people were selfish and were not likely to put their country ahead of themselves, despite the fact that many of them had done just that in fighting the Revolution, struggling to write the Constitution, and forming the new government. Hamilton was convinced that people had to be given personal incentives to work for the general good. His program was meant to do that.

Congress did not accept Hamilton's scheme entirely. But it did approve of the key points. The national debt was funded as Hamilton wished, and interest was paid on it; and the Bank of the United States was set up.

While we may believe that Hamilton's plans were not always democratic and that they helped one class of people more than others, there is no doubt that he was a brilliant and far-seeing man. His programs almost instantly put the new United States on a sound financial footing and laid the platform from which the country rocketed to prosperity.

CHAPTER III

The Whiskey Rebellion

The new government depended for its income almost entirely on import duties on goods coming into the country and excise taxes on goods sold within the country. We still pay excise taxes today on many products, like whiskey, cigarettes, luxury goods, and even gasoline: If you look at the price signs in gas stations you will see how much of the price is a government tax.

The question always is, What should be taxed? Generally it is believed that necessities like food ought not to be taxed, but nonessential goods, like cigarettes and perfumes, can be. People thought much the same in Hamilton's time, and he decided to lay an excise tax on whiskey. It was not an essential item (although most people drank it), and furthermore, he wanted everybody to share the expense of running the national government, not just importers in the port cities.

The people most affected by the tax on whiskey were the western farmers in the areas lying across the Appalachian Mountain chain—western New York, Pennsylvania, and some of the southern states. The farmers of western Pennsylvania were particularly hard hit by the whiskey tax. Their primary export crop was grain. It was very difficult to cart huge wagonloads of wheat or corn a hundred or more miles over rough dirt roads, and even worse across the Appalachians to eastern seaports, like Philadelphia, where it could be sold. It was far easier to distill the grain into whiskey, reducing a wagon-load of rye or wheat or barley into a keg of whiskey. The people of western Pennsylvania felt that they had no choice but to reduce their grain and corn to whiskey, and that the tax on it was therefore unfair. The whiskey tax was passed in March 1791, and almost immediately there were protests. The Pennsylvania legislature took up resolutions against it, and in the western part of the state there were noisy meetings to oppose it.

But Washington, Hamilton, and the majority in Congress were determined to collect the tax, and the collectors went forth to do so. Hamilton had something else in the back of his mind. He believed that a government would not be respected until it had proved its strength by a show of force.

The Pennsylvania farmers gave him the chance to make his show of force. They tarred and feathered some of the tax collectors; and when that did not do the trick, they beat up their neighbors who were paying the tax and shot holes in their stills.

Hamilton was all for raising the militia and rushing out to the area of rebellion to arrest its leaders and bring them to trial. But Washington, as ever thoughtful, decided merely to issue a proclamation calling on the rebels to obey the law. Through 1792 and into 1793, the scrap simmered along. Then in June 1793, Washington and Hamilton decided to clamp down and had writs served on a number of the rebels. The rebels resisted. Finally, in July 1794, a mob of five hundred angry farmers gathered at the house of the main tax collector in Allegheny County. A few soldiers came to defend the house, and a couple of members of the mob—including their commander—were killed. The tax collector managed to escape with his family, and the mob burned down his house.

A couple of weeks later some six thousand protesters gathered near

A cartoon showing a government whiskey inspector being tarred, feathered, and ridden on a rail, while local Pennsylvania farmers jeer.

Pittsburgh, threatening a rebellion. This was too much even for Washington, who had hoped to find a peaceful solution. He called up the militia and put together an army of twelve thousand men. This was a far larger force than was necessary for the job—a real show of force. Once the rebels saw what they were up against, they melted away and thereafter paid the whiskey tax. In the end, only a few of the ringleaders were arrested, and Washington eventually pardoned them. He had made his point—that the people had to obey the laws, however unfair they might seem to some.

In fact, the western farmers had less to complain about the national government than it appeared. Between 1790 and 1796, well over 80 percent of the entire national budget was being spent fighting the Indians on the western frontier the farmers had pushed into. The battling between Indians and whites over land in America right from the beginning raises a great many questions of right and wrong that still trouble people today. The first European settlers did not doubt that they had a right to come into what they saw as underused land. The Indians, who could easily have driven out the people in the tiny early colonies, like Jamestown and Plymouth, chose not to, mostly because they wanted to trade for European goods, especially weapons. By the time they realized that the Europeans were taking over their land, it was too late. (Readers interested in the European takeover of America can find more detail in *The Clash of Cultures*, the first book in this series.)

By the early 1800s, the Indians on lands across the Appalachian Mountains had decided to make a stand. This lithograph shows Indians battling American troops outside a fort in the wilderness.

Many of the European settlers thought all along that the Indians ought to be treated fairly; but many others did not care. As settlers continued to pour in from Europe, especially the British Isles, simple population pressures pushed them farther and farther west. By 1790, the Indians had decided to stand firm against the whites at the Ohio River. They were supported by the British in their outposts around the Great Lakes. At battles in 1790 and 1791, the Indians attacked American forces and beat them badly.

Over the next few years, the Indians continued to raid white settlements, burning isolated farms and sometimes massacring whole families, men, women, and children. Terrified whites fought back, massacring Indians in turn.

In 1794, the government sent a Revolutionary War hero, General "Mad" Anthony Wayne, with a strong force into the western territory. Wayne crushed the Indians in the Battle of Fallen Timbers. The Indians, discouraged, agreed to a treaty, sold the U.S. government a huge chunk of land for $10,000, and backed off.

General "Mad" Anthony Wayne, a hero of the Revolution, had scored a triumph at Stoney Point on the Hudson River and led troops in the final American victory at Yorktown. Wayne beat the Indians in the Battle of Fallen Timbers, and he effectively ended them as a power in the area south of Lake Erie.

Effectively, the Indian threat had been removed from a substantial part of the area south of Lake Erie to the Ohio River, and the region rapidly began to fill up.

The new government had, by this time, established its credits and American capitalists had built up industry and commerce, in no small part because of Hamilton's financial policies. Now, with the defeat of the whiskey rebels and the Indians, the federal government had shown that it had enough power to keep the peace in its lands.

CHAPTER IV

Foreign Problems

What is now the United States had originally been settled by several powerful European nations. The English had occupied most of the seacoast from the Carolinas into Maine. The French had settled what is now, roughly, Canada. The Dutch had taken over portions of New York State and made forays into Connecticut. The Spanish had established outposts in present-day Florida and areas around it.

These were maritime nations, who were growing rich and powerful through their fleets of cargo ships and the colonies they were developing to fill the ships with goods—silks and spices from the Far East; sugar from the Caribbean Islands; tobacco, timber, codfish, furs, and much else from North America. These maritime nations saw the colonies as being there primarily for the benefit of Europeans. The colonies were, in a sense, captive lands that were supposed to supply the goods that would make their European masters rich.

The colonies that would become the United States were thus tied tightly to European nations, principally England, for 170 years before the Revolution. That is a long time—many of the people living during the

Revolution had had great-grandfathers born in America. Americans had for all these generations been twisting and turning in the harness that attached them to European nations, and most of them assumed that Europe was not out to do them much good.

But even as the new government was being established, the ties to at least two European countries remained strong. For one, most Americans spoke English, read English books, followed English manners, had developed their religions out of English ones, and most important, built their colonial governments with their individual rights and freedoms on English models. However angry Americans might be with the English because of the Revolution, they also admired English power and English

In building their new government, Americans had frequently looked to English institutions, with which they had been familiar for two centuries. Although American leaders were often at odds with the British Parliament, it was the model for American state legislatures and, to some extent, the Congress. In this painting, the great English statesman William Pitt the Younger addresses Parliament.

Americans were also impressed by British power and wealth. Here a wealthy English family poses in its drawing room while a couple dances to an oboe. Many rich Americans modeled their manners and behavior on English customs like these.

culture. George Washington habitually sent to England for clothes, books, furniture; some of his family had actually gone to live there. Alexander Hamilton's father had been born a British citizen. Hamilton much admired English ways. Another of the major political leaders, John Adams, had spent many years in London as America's representative there. He, too, felt that there was much to admire in England.

But France also had a claim on American affections. True, during the 1750s Americans had fought alongside the British to drive the French out of America in the French and Indian War. But the French had provided critically important help to the Americans against the British during the Revolution. During the war, the Americans and French had signed a treaty committing them each to help the other in time of war. The French, of course, were not acting only out of a spirit of friendship; they had their

French support was critical in helping the Americans win the Revolution. The young Marquis de Lafayette was much celebrated for his devotion to the American cause and for his help in organizing American troops. In this paint-ing by the famous artist Thomas Rossiter, George Washington (right) is shown greeting Lafayette at Washington's home in Virginia.

own reasons for aiding the United States. Nonetheless, they were friends.

American love of the French was increased in 1789 when the French people revolted, and threw off the king and nobles who had been run-ning the country for centuries. It seemed to Americans that they and the French had made common cause in search of freedom from tyranny. When the French Revolution turned into a bloodbath, with thousands of people, many of them innocent of any wrongdoing, losing their heads to the guillotine, American stomachs grew queasy, and many people turned against the French. But a surprising amount of good feeling toward France remained.

European nations felt differently. Kings, queens, princes, prime min-isters watched in horror as French dukes, counts, and finally the king and queen lost their heads, and soon enough European statesmen began to form an alliance to bring down the revolutionary government in France and put a king back on the throne.

England in particular was determined to crush France. England and France had been battling off and on since the 1300s; many of the most famous battles in history, like Poitiers, Agincourt, Crécy, the Plains of Abraham, and in the nineteenth century Waterloo, were fought between the English and the French. There was a natural antipathy between the nations.

The French Revolution began in 1789, the same year that Washington took office as our first president. By 1792, the French were at war with Austria and Prussia. In January of 1793, the revolutionary French government beheaded its king and queen. Soon afterward the British joined the war against France, and in time Holland and Spain were drawn in.

The question for Washington and his government was what to do. Some people, like Thomas Jefferson, who had spent a good deal of time in France as the American representative there, sympathized strongly with the democratic ideals of the French revolutionaries, despite all the bloodshed and beheadings. Others, like Washington and Hamilton, who liked the idea of strong central government, were dismayed by the chaos spreading through France. They had always favored the English in the conflict with France and continued to do so. Soon factions developed around these differing points of view on the English-French war.

Both factions agreed that the United States ought to stay out of the war. However, that was easier said than done. Naturally, neither the French nor the English wanted the Americans to sell the enemy food and other supplies; but of course the Americans wanted to be free to sell anything they wanted to either side. At the time, there existed a complex set of rules about how neutral countries could trade with "belligerents" (nations at war). There were other questions involved, too, like whether warships of either side could put in to neutral ports—in this case Boston,

Many American were disillusioned with the French cause when the French Revolution became a bloodbath, with the guillotine clanging incessantly. This picture shows the beheading of Louis XVI.

New York, Philadelphia—for repairs and supplies. In actual fact, both the French and the English were violating the rules of war right along, capturing American vessels and their cargoes, sometimes even "impressing" sailors from American ships and putting them to work on their own ships. That is, if a sailor on an American ship could not prove he was American, the English captain would say he was an English deserter and take him away to serve in the British navy.

In making his decision, Washington was faced with the inconvenient fact that America had a mutual defense pact with France, which required either country to help the other in case of attack. What to do about this treaty proved to be the main point of the argument between the two factions developing over the war. Hamilton and those who sided with the English wanted the United States to at least temporarily "suspend" the treaty. Jefferson argued that suspending the treaty would be not only immoral, but an open act of aggression against France.

The final decision was up to George Washington. The president was not a philosopher like Jefferson, nor a brilliant and imaginative political thinker like Hamilton. He was nonetheless very astute. He always asked for advice from the people he trusted most; then he carefully weighed everything in his mind and almost always came to the most sensible decision. He did so in this case. He decided against suspending the treaty with France. He would just see how things worked out—no point in borrowing trouble, as we would say today. He then issued his famous Neutrality Proclamation. It said that the United States would "adopt and pursue a conduct friendly and impartial toward the belligerent powers." The Neutrality Proclamation also warned Americans not to aid or abet any of the warring nations, at risk of being prosecuted by the U.S. government.

This was a powerful statement, and over the remainder of his time in office, Washington worked diligently to hold to this policy of neutrality. In so doing he stated principles of American foreign policy that presidents aspired to through the nineteenth century and into the twentieth. Later on he summed up his ideas about foreign policy in a few words. The United States was to "observe good faith and justice toward all nations. Cultivate peace and harmony with all." But the country should also "steer clear of permanent alliances with any portion of the foreign world." It must also be prepared to defend itself against foreign meddling, by which he was taken to mean encroachments not only on the United States but on areas around it as well. Although Europe was thrown into war again and again through the nineteenth century, the United States stayed clear. Even when America began to play a larger role in the world in the twentieth century, the temper of the nation still was to "steer clear" of foreign entanglements. Only in Latin America and the Far East did the U.S. government become involved in other nations' affairs. The nation did send troops to Europe to fight in the later stages of World War I, but as soon as that war was over, Americans pulled back, refusing even to join the League of Nations, the forerunner to today's United Nations. Not until the Japanese bombed Pearl Harbor in 1941, and drew the country into World War II, did the United States finally fully abandon the policy set by Washington and commit itself to playing a role on the world stage, as it has done ever since. Once again the new government had laid out a track that the country would follow.

But it was one thing to set a neutral course; it was quite another to stick to it, with winds buffeting the sails from several directions at once. One key problem was that the British, whether Americans liked it or not, were still holding some forts in the Great Lakes area. Their presence encouraged the Indians in what was known as the Northwest Territory to harass American settlers coming over the mountains. It also allowed the British to control the very lucrative fur trade with the Indians there.

Another problem was that the British were still refusing to let American shippers trade with their islands in the Caribbean. This West Indian trade had always been important to American merchants and the farmers whose grain, meat, and other commodities West Indians bought. Worse, much of the federal government's income came from duties on imports, and the nation's biggest trading partner was England. Beyond all of this, Hamilton was emotionally drawn to England, just as Jefferson was drawn to France.

On top of everything, the British navy was stopping American ships that might be bringing supplies to the enemy French and frequently impressing American sailors. American tempers against the British were rising, and there was much talk of war.

Washington saw clearly that these problems had to be solved, and in

1794 he sent the New Yorker John Jay to London to see if he could settle some of these matters. Jay was a man experienced in government and diplomacy. He brought back a treaty that opened up trade with the British West Indies in a very limited way and got the British to promise to withdraw from their Great Lakes forts. Jay's Treaty covered some other matters as well, but it did nothing about the impressment of American sailors nor about other issues that concerned various groups of Americans. Many Americans hated Jay's Treaty for different reasons, but Washington believed it was probably the best deal he could get. In fact, he recognized that without some kind of a settlement, America might find itself at war with the British again. He urged the Senate to ratify the treaty, and reluctantly, the Senate did.

The fracas over Jay's Treaty had two results, besides settling some of the issues between England and

John Jay was one of the most skillful diplomats in the early period of the United States. The treaty Jay negotiated with the British, to stop harassment of American shipping during England's war with France, was probably the best that could be expected. Many Americans, though, felt that Jay had given up too much.

the United States and avoiding war. For one, during the debates, the House of Representatives asked Washington for papers relating to the treaty. Washington refused to turn them over, "because of the necessity of maintaining the boundaries fixed by the Constitution." In other words, in Washington's opinion the separation of powers did not allow the Congress to examine the president's confidential papers. This principle of "executive privilege" is claimed by presidents today.

Once again we can see how this first government under the Constitution, in the process of dealing with the real problems it faced, established precedents and principles that would become fixed policy for succeeding generations of Americans. Another important element of the American system of government that grew by practice rather than developing out of provisions in the Constitution itself is the two-party system. We must now turn our attention to that "mixed blessing."

CHAPTER V

The Rise of Political Parties

Political parties today play such an essential role in making our American democracy work that it is hard to imagine our government functioning without them. This is especially true in view of the fact that Washington and the men he chose to help run the government hated the idea and practice of party politics. Indeed, once the Constitution had been ratified in 1788, the old rivalry between those opposed and those in favor of adopting the Constitution faded away, and it looked for a moment as if the United States would have a harmonious one-party—or even no-party- –system.

But differences over policy matters were bound to arise; and perhaps not surprisingly, one group of people found themselves in agreement on range of very different issues, while opposing another group of people who agreed among themselves on the other side of the issues. In other words, political parties just came about without anyone organizing them at the start, because people with similar ideas and attitudes about the direction the United States should take joined together to oppose those with a different version of America's future.

Why, since the Founding Fathers—Washington, Madison, Jefferson,

Political parties are so much a part of the American culture that it is hard to see how the political system would work without them in United States history. They took shape very early. Right, ribbons in support of candidates Clay, Polk, and Fillmore in the election of 1844.

Left, the twentieth-century version of the ribbons —campaign buttons in support of Al Smith in the 1928 election, Harry Truman (1948), and Adlai Stevenson (1956).

Adams, and the rest—so despised political parties, did they arise and become central to our political way of life?

The answer lies as much as any place in the dispute over Jay's Treaty and the division between "Anglophiles"—literally lovers of England— and Francophiles. It was here that the bitter rhetoric of party rivalry became intense, even hate-filled. But, of course, the roots of the division lay deep in the conflict over Hamilton's plan for developing a commercial and industrial nation and the Bank of the United States, and deeper still in varying philosophies about how best to secure the American people a free and prosperous future.

By the 1790s, Americans had been to a considerable extent running their own affairs for over a century and a half. In that time they had fought step by step to gain rights and freedoms that few people anywhere else in the world had, or could even think of having. In most places kings, queens, and their aristocratic supporters held life-and-death power over the mass of people. The English people had managed to gain certain rights for themselves, and the French, in their recent revolution, had thrown off some of the weight of their rulers. But a special sun shone on Americans. Rights and freedoms we exercise so casually today were very precious to those early Americans, who saw how rare they were elsewhere.

People like Washington, Hamilton, and their supporters believed as much as anyone in the rights of Americans; many of them had, after all, helped to write the Constitution and the Bill of Rights, which set forth those rights. (For the story of the creation of the Constitution and the Bill of Rights, see *Creating the Constitution*, the sixth book of this series.) But Washington, Hamilton, and their allies were believers in strong government. This belief in strong government was based in part on their idea that the common people did not have the patience or expertise to solve the kinds of knotty problems any government faces. Surprisingly, a good many ordinary people agreed. America was still to some extent what historians call a "deferential" society. Ordinary people were not going to let their leaders trample on their hard-won rights; nonetheless, they believed they ought to show respect for richer, often better-educated people of the upper class, and they were more willing to take direction from them than would be the case today.

It therefore seemed natural to many people, especially among the wealthy, that some were meant to lead and some were meant to follow. Ordinary people, so this thinking went, did not have enough education and experience of the world to make wise decisions in large matters of public policy. Once people had elected their government, they ought to do what it said without grumbling. If citizens didn't like the policies of their government, they could chose a new one when the next elections came around.

George Washington was one who followed this line of thinking. In his Farewell Address he said that it is "the duty of every individual to obey the established government." He even believed that the people should not form "combinations and associations"—what we would today call pressure groups—to push government in various ways.

Washington's right-hand man, Secretary of the Treasury Alexander Hamilton, was an even more devout believer in strong government. As we have seen, he felt it was in the best interests of the United States for the wealthy merchants, manufacturers, exporters, and importers not merely to have a free hand to enrich themselves further, but actually to receive various kinds of government support. In doing business, so Hamilton thought, these merchants would bring prosperity to everybody else—jobs for sailors and fishermen, markets for farmers with corn and hogs to sell.

Hamilton and Washington were not alone in holding these opinions. They had the support of many Americans, both small farmers and leading figures like Vice President John Adams; the first chief justice, John Jay; Attorney General Edmund Randolph. Taken together, these leaders believed in strong central government, fairly weak state governments, a

The brilliant Alexander Hamilton was profoundly important in establishing the United States commercial system and in putting the government on a sound footing right from the start. Hamilton believed in government by a talented and principled elite. He felt that once the people had elected their officials, they should follow their lead.

deferential populace, and policies that would suit the interests of merchants, shippers, big plantation owners. Indeed, they had a certain fondness for the formalities and ceremonies that had always existed around the British monarch and his court. Washington liked to hold formal parties at which everybody was elegantly dressed. Some of his supporters even wanted the president to be addressed as "Your Excellency," or even "Your Majesty," although this went too far for Washington, who insisted on "Mr. President," the title we still use today.

The people who sided with Washington, Hamilton, and others came to be called "Federalists," at least partly because they favored a strong federal government. They were not organized into a political party in the modern sense—there was no "Federalist headquarters," no chairman of the Federalist Party, no campaign buttons or slogans, certainly no

Like Hamilton, George Washington believed in leadership by an elite. As president, he regularly gave formal parties for visitors and dignitaries. At these events he always dressed elegantly, as in this portrait by the celebrated painter Charles Willson Peale.

Federalist convention to nominate candidates for president. But these people shared ideas, met with each other, wrote letters to each other setting forth their ideas, supported each other, and pushed their ideas in newspapers favorable to them—or, in fact, started newspapers to publicize their policies. The Federalists, then, were not a political party in the modern sense—indeed, they would not have wanted to think of themselves as members of a political party.

Not surprisingly, there were many Americans who did not like the ideas of Washington, Hamilton, and their Federalist friends.

Chief among them were two figures as important to our history as the Federalist leaders: Thomas Jefferson and James Madison. Both men were what we would call geniuses. Jefferson had one of those great minds that touched upon everything. He played the violin, designed his famous home, Monticello, himself, and filled it with curious inventions, like a device that would make a copy of a letter as he wrote it. He was owner of a large plantation, and thus had a professional interest in agriculture, but he also studied nature deeply and was always collecting seeds from strange plants to grow in his gardens. He was a philosopher, reading and writing widely. He would certainly have been chosen to go to the Constitutional Convention in 1787, except that at the time he represented the American government in Paris. He was truly an all-around man.

Thomas Jefferson strongly believed that the heart and soul of America lay in the ordinary people, most especially the small farmers and their families who made up the bulk of the nation. Because they owned their own farms—free of bosses and landlords—and grew or made at home almost everything they needed,

Thomas Jefferson, shown here in a portrait by Peale, and his friend James Madison disagreed with Hamilton. According to Jefferson and his followers, the "plain people," the farm families who made up the vast majority of Americans, could be trusted to do what was right.

Jefferson was a remarkable man—a philosopher, politician, inventor, student of science. His library included books in Latin, German, French, and many other languages.

they could be independent; and because they were independent, they were incorruptible. Jefferson wrote, "Corruption of morals in the mass of cultivators is a phenomenon of which no age nor nation has furnished an example." To the contrary, he believed, those who manufactured goods for sale were dependent on "casualties and caprice of customers."

Europeans needed factories and mills because there was not enough land for every family to have an independent farm. But in America there was plenty of land, so, said Jefferson, let Americans grow food and import what manufactured goods they needed from Europe. Cities, it naturally followed, were corrupt, because they were populated by exploitative manufacturers and workers dependent on their bosses who might feel they had to vote as their bosses told them.

Jefferson's ally James Madison echoed Jefferson's ideas when he wrote, "The class of citizens [farmers] who provide at once their own food and their own raiment, may be viewed as the most truly independent and happy. They are more: they are the best basis of public liberty, and the strongest bulwark of public safety." Cities, he added, were overcrowded and filled with "distresses and vices."

Jefferson and Madison believed that cities were chronic cesspools, filled with evil. One of the dominating buildings in Philadelphia was the Walnut Street jail, then just behind Independence Hall. People walking past the jail, including the Founding Fathers on the way to the hall to write the Constitution, were often showered with insults and curses as they went by.

This viewpoint may sound a little comical today, when huge numbers of Americans live in cities a hundred times larger than the ones Jefferson and Madison knew. But it is true that there were in the cities of that time a lot of petty criminals, beggars, and such—people who did not seem to be doing much for the welfare of the nation.

Adding it up, we easily see that it was not just disagreement about whether to support the French or the English in their war that divided Washington and the Federalists from Jefferson and his allies: They were opposed on many philosophic and political points. Jefferson, Madison, and their group quickly found a name for themselves: Republicans. (The modern Republican Party dates from the mid-nineteenth century and is not descended from this one.) The Republicans supported the French; the

Federalists supported the English. The Republicans wanted to base the new nation on farmers and buy manufactured goods from other nations, to avoid the corrupting effects of factories; the Federalists were all for commerce and determined to build an American manufacturing system. The Republicans thought that the Federal government should interfere in the affairs of the states as little as possible; the Federalists, as their name suggests, were in favor of strong national government at the expense of the state governments. Finally, the Republicans trusted those sensible, self-sufficient farmers to make wise decisions about things; the Federalists, at least so the Republicans believed, wanted to establish some sort of aristocracy that would be the natural enemy of democracy; and it is true that many Federalists did not trust the wisdom of the people but believed that the people ought to put the government into the hands of men of talent, energy, and intelligence who would know best what to do.

The great irony is that Republicans and Federalists both believed that political parties were evil. They had seen the Tories and the Whigs in England go at each other, and they were convinced that parties always looked out for themselves, regardless of what was best for the country. The Republicans and Federalists were certainly not parties in the modern sense; but they disliked each other as much as people in modern parties do and, as we shall shortly see, were ready to fight tooth and nail to keep the other side out of power.

Political parties, then, are another major element of our governmental system, along with the cabinet and—as we shall see—judicial review, which we might call "extraconstitutional." They are legal, essential, and of long and unbroken tradition, but are nowhere mentioned in the Constitution.

Washington's Farewell

George Washington was a man who loved nothing better than being home tending to his great plantation. He had a large old house, Mount Vernon, which we can visit today. He had bought for it fine furniture, glasses, silverware. He entertained constantly. Overnight visitors stayed there much of the time, and he once said that he had not sat down to dinner alone with his wife for twenty years. Often there would be ten people at his table. Wealthy people of that day were expected to entertain frequently. But Washington was a man who truly liked having other people around.

Even more, he liked to get up early in the morning and ride around his estate, seeing what needed to be done and giving orders to his stewards. He liked improving things—putting in an orchard, having a new barn built, trying a new type of seed.

Yet he had spent much of his life away from his beloved home. He had fought in the French and Indian War during the 1750s, when he was a young man. Between 1775 and 1783, he had been leading the American army in the Revolution, and in 1787, after after a few years at home, he had gone to Philadelphia, where he served as president of the

Constitutional Convention. He spent the next year fighting to get his home state of Virginia to ratify the Constitution, and the eight years following in New York and Philadelphia as president of the nation. He was tired of it all, tired of the factional fighting between Federalists and Republicans, tired of dealing with the foolish and self-serving people any president is faced with. He had, once, been revered by the American people to an extent that no president has been since. But the political battling had inevitably spilled over on him, as he was forced to take sides on issues, and he found himself being attacked, even insulted, in the newspapers. By 1796, he was fed up, and he wanted to go home.

An artist's re-creation of George Washington at home on his plantation, directing workers, mainly slaves, as they harvest the hay. This lithograph, made in 1853 from an earlier painting, shows plantation life to be a good deal more idyllic than it was. However, Washington proved a kind master, and his slaves were undoubtedly better off than many others.

Washington's beloved home, Mount Vernon, has been preserved as a national shrine. Here it is as it was in the middle of the twentieth century.

The Constitution did not set any limit on how many terms a president might serve, and many people expected that Washington would go on being reelected until he died in office. The very idea chilled his heart. He had, in fact, wanted to give up the presidency after his first four years, but the new government was still trying to find its way, and he had been persuaded to serve a second term. By 1796, Washington was adamant: He was going to retire to enjoy his final years at peace on his farm.

In refusing to run for a third term he set a precedent that presidents followed for almost 150 years. After all, if the great George Washington refused a third term, what lesser mortal would dare to run for one? No one did until 1940 when Franklin D. Roosevelt broke the tradition; he was elected for a fourth term in 1944. (In 1951 the twenty-second amendment limiting presidents to two full terms was added to the Constitution.) The ironic part of it is that Washington never intended to set the two-term precedent when he retired. While he may have felt that no president should serve for too long—and certainly should not stay in office until he died—the main point was that Washington simply wanted to go home and live out his days in peace.

But before he did so, Washington wanted to give his fellow Americans some advice, indeed warnings, based on what he had learned in starting up the new government. He never actually delivered his famous Farewell Address as a speech, but gave it to the newspapers to be published.

The Farewell Address takes up two basic subjects, foreign affairs and domestic affairs. The part concerning foreign affairs concluded the Address and made a relatively simple point: that the United States ought to "steer clear of permanent alliances with any portion of the foreign world." We must understand that in the late eighteenth century, and for a long time before and after, the relatively small European nations, set against each other cheek by jowl, were constantly forming and breaking alliances in various combinations for defense or attack. Washington was not against waging war when it was necessary; he had, after all, led the American forces during the Revolution. But he recognized that the United States was still struggling to its feet and had many problems to solve. It was better not to be drawn into conflicts if they could be avoided, at least not until the country had become more powerful.

The other section of the Farewell Address appeared, on the face of it, to be equally straightforward. Americans ought, he said, to beware of the spirit of "party." Parties "put in place of the delegated will of the nation, the will of a party, often a small but artful and enterprising minority of the community." Washington, we remember, was not talking about political parties in the modern sense, which did not exist in 1796, but about what we would call "factions," or even "pressure groups." And it is certainly true that governments today are pressed hard by groups seeking to advance their own selfish interests regardless of the good of the nation as a whole.

But to historians, reading between the lines, there was more to it than that. Like most honest people who are elected to public office, Washington had thought very carefully about his policies, about what the government should do. He had become firmly convinced that his ideas were so logical and obvious that nobody with any common sense could oppose them. But in many cases people did oppose them. They could only be doing this, Washington believed, because they were at best wrong-headed and at worst trying to "direct, control, counteract" the policies of the government for the welfare of all, and turn them to their own selfish ends. Washington had always thought that he was trying to pull the com-

Election day in Philadelphia in 1815. At extreme left, two men fight on a doorstep, presumably over politics. At center, a drunken man is being helped to the polls by a politician. Other groups quarrel over the merits of their candidates. Washington deplored this spirit of "party," which he thought produced disorder and strife.

peting Republican and Federalist factions together, staying above the battle himself. But most historians believe that he was basically in sympathy with the Federalist position. They thus feel that the Farewell Address was to some extent a campaign speech, urging Americans to support his policies, which were more Federalist than Republican.

George Washington's Farewell Address has continued to be quoted even to this day, particularly on the point that the country ought to steer clear of too much involvement with foreign nations. That idea was the basis of American foreign policy in regard to European affairs for a century between the War of 1812 and World War I. We cannot say he alone set the policy, but his words were often quoted in support of it by others who thought it wise.

The Administration of John Adams

George Washington was going to retire, and who would be the next president? The Federalists quickly settled on John Adams, who had been Washington's vice president, an important figure among the Massachusetts rebels twenty years earlier and an experienced diplomat who had served as America's representative in England. The Republicans had two very strong possibilities: Thomas Jefferson, who had been Washington's secretary of state, and James Madison, the most influential delegate at the Constitutional Convention. Jefferson got the support of the Republicans. Once again we must remember that these were not political parties in the modern sense. They were instead factions—groups of people adhering to similar ideas, who were in touch with one another about policies and politics.

Alexander Hamilton, the Federalist leader, was imperious and abrasive, not popular enough to be elected himself. The Federalists, however, were not unified behind Adams. Hamilton, for one, felt that Adams was too strong a man in his own right to be controlled, and he schemed to throw Federalist votes to another candidate.

The main issue in the campaign of 1796 was the war between

John Adams, from Massachusetts, was one of the great leaders who founded the American republic. He served as American emissary to England, as Washington's vice president, and then as president. He was a staunch Federalist, like Washington and Hamilton.

England and France. Despite the regular doleful clanging of the guillotine in Paris, the Republicans continued to side with France, partly because they carried a long-standing hatred for the old enemy—England—and partly out of sympathy for the French revolutionary spirit. In the view of the Republicans, England was a decadent nation ruled by a ruthless government wholly antidemocratic in spirit. Jefferson, the Republicans' favorite, was sure that the French would soon invade England and send the king and prime minister into exile; and he went on believing for years that the British people were about to revolt.

Jefferson had been American minister to France, while Adams was representing the United States in England. Adams, like many Americans, was horrified by the bloody turn the French Revolution had taken. From both political and personal conviction, he favored England and hoped to improve relations with the English.

American voters preferred the Federalists, but because of Hamilton's scheming, Adams barely squeaked in over Jefferson. Under the rule at the time, Jefferson, with the second largest number of electoral votes, became vice president.

Inevitably, Adams's first problem was the war between the French and the English. As much as Washington had wanted the United States to stay out of European affairs, there was in this case no way to do so. American prosperity was heavily dependent on exporting its farm products, codfish, timber to Europe and the West Indies, which were largely controlled by European powers.

In the Battle of the Nile, the English destroyed much of the French fleet. Thereafter, Britain controlled the seas to a large extent. As a result, England could treat American shipping any way it wanted. The picture here is an engraving from an artist's interpretation of the battle.

As we have seen, the rules of war in respect to neutral nations were routinely broken by both the French and the English. the controversial Jay's Treaty of 1794 had seemed to many Americans, and certainly to the Republicans, to tip the country toward England. The French took the treaty as an insult, and they began capturing American ships and their cargoes with whatever excuse they could dream up. Before the Adams administration ended in 1801, the French had captured 1,853 American ships and their cargoes, worth over seven million dollars, an amount that would run into billions in today's money. (The British had actually captured over ten million dollars worth of American ships and cargoes before Jay's Treaty was ratified in 1795.)

Americans were angry, especially the shippers and shipowners who were suffering from French attacks, and there was talk of war with France. But Adams remained cool—among other things he knew that many Americans supported the French Revolution. He sent a delegation to Paris to work out rules for neutral shipping. The French government, however, had been led to believe that support for France in America was much stronger than it actually was. Furthermore, the French minister of foreign affairs was Charles-Maurice de Talleyrand, a corrupt and high-handed politician, whose very name today suggests secrets, whispers, and intrigue. He not only treated the American envoys like peasants, but insisted that they pay him a huge bribe before he would even receive them in his offices.

The American envoys were shocked and angry. When word got back to President Adams, he responded with strong words, and set about getting ready for war. The Republicans were dismayed, and refused to believe that their friends the French would behave this way. Jefferson insisted that Adams make the diplomatic papers and the letters about the affair public. Adams did so, and the Republicans were forced to shut up: However much many Americans liked the French, they were Americans first and would not tolerate being insulted. Very quickly, Congress autho-

This cartoon shows the three American ministers (at left) resisting demands by corrupt French officials for money. The four-headed French monster is saying, "We must have money, plenty of money." The American responds, "Cease bawling, Monster! We will not give you six pence." Americans were outraged by French demands for bribes.

rized the building of a war fleet. Washington agreed to leave his beloved Mount Vernon to lead another army if it came to war. Trade with France came to a halt, and the American government looked for ways to improve relations with England. American ships, both official naval vessels and private ones, began capturing French ships.

Meanwhile, in a move that would have tremendous consequences for the United States, back in France the double-dealing Talleyrand was try-

Two of the American delegates to France who finally worked out a deal to end French attacks on American ships. At left, the chief justice of the Supreme Court, Oliver Ellsworth; at right, North Carolina governor William R. Davie. John Adams's coolness in avoiding war with the French was a high point in his administration.

ing to gain control of the Louisiana territory. Louisiana included not only New Orleans, but most of the enormous piece of land between the Mississippi River and the Rocky Mountains, roughly *half* of today's United States. The French had originally settled New Orleans and, during the time they held Canada, had set up forts and trading posts along the Mississippi. On the strength of this they claimed the Louisiana territory. The land had been turned over to Spain in an earlier deal; but now Talleyrand had the idea of developing a great colonial empire in the area around the Mississippi, and he wanted the Louisiana territory back. If France were at war with the United States, however, Americans could easily sweep away new settlements across the Mississippi.

For a variety of reasons, then, Talleyrand decided to back down. Adams sent a new set of envoys to France, and a deal was worked out, setting up the rules for the shipping of neutral nations. The French stopped attacking American vessels. Washington had managed to avoid war with England through Jay's Treaty, and now Adams had managed to avoid war with France through a similar agreement. Keeping the peace was probably the most significant achievement of Adams's administration. It was an important one, for the last thing the United States needed at that point was another war. The young nation now had a little breathing space in which to grow. Politically, however, it was costly to Adams, for many Americans had wanted war with France. It took courage on Adams's part to follow this sensible neutral course.

The political struggle between the Federalists and the Republicans over whether to favor England or France in the European war had one consequence that has continued to echo down American history for over two hundred years. This was the passage of the Alien and Sedition Acts. (An *alien* is an immigrant who has not become a citizen; *sedition* means to stir up trouble against the government.)

The problem was that President John Adams and his Federalists still could not see that American politicians were now divided into two parties, and that the Federalists were one of them. Adams, Hamilton, and their followers believed, like Washington, that they were working hard to do their best for the United States, and from their point of view, they certainly were. They believed that anyone who was fighting for policies different from theirs was doing so only because they wanted to take over or, worse, to advance the interests of a foreign power, in this case, France.

Adams and the Federalist Congress decided they had to defend the United States against foreign influence. Actually, Adams himself was not enthusiastic about the Alien and Sedition Acts, but he allowed himself to be swept along by those who were. The acts allowed the U.S. government to deport aliens whom it considered "dangerous," which essentially meant French ones and the Irish who often sided with them. (The Irish had been hostile to the English for centuries and traditionally sided with the enemies of England.) When it came down to it, however, the Adams government never actually deported anyone.

It was the Sedition Act that caused trouble. It allowed the government to prosecute anyone who spoke or published "any false, scandalous, and malicious" statement against the government, Congress, or the president. In effect, the law would prevent the Republicans from criticizing the Federalists in power. Under it, twenty-five people were arrested, and ten were actually sent to the jail. The most famous of these cases was against the Republican congressman Matthew Lyon, who edited a newspaper in Vermont. Lyon was fined $1,000, worth at least $100,000 in today's money, and was sent to jail.

The Federalists insisted that the Sedition Act was fair under the Constitution, because if somebody like Matthew Lyon could prove that his criticisms of government were true and that he hadn't acted maliciously, he would get off. But many people disagreed, and most historians disagree today: The Sedition Act does appear to go against the freedom of speech clause in the Bill of Rights. The problem is this: Suppose you were to write, "The government in Washington today is all for the rich and doesn't do anything for people with low incomes." A statement like that might or might not be true, but you would have a hard time proving it. More significant, a law like the Sedition Act threw the "burden of proof" on the accused person. It is a very basic rule of law that the accused person does not have to prove his or her innocence; it is up to the prosecution to prove that the person is guilty. But the Sedition Act forced the accused person to prove that what he or she said was true.

Probably the majority of Americans were not happy about the Alien and Sedition Acts. The Republicans of course hated them, for they saw that the acts were aimed at them, as of course they were. Indeed, Republicans were convinced that the Sedition Act was unconstitutional,

In 1797, Republican Congressman Matthew Lyon from Vermont spat in the face of Federalist Roger Griswold, congressman from Connecticut, and a fight broke out. Not surprisingly, the tempestuous "Spitting" Lyon, as he was henceforth known, was one of the chief victims of the Alien and Sedition Acts. Because of disparaging remarks he wrote about Federalist president Adams, Lyon was brought to trial. He insisted that the Sedition Act was unconstitutional. It probably was, but he was jailed anyway for four months and fined $1,000, a large sum for the time.

that Congress had violated the free speech and free press clauses of the First Amendment. But how could citizens legally overturn an act of Congress? One theory was that the Constitution was a compact of the state governments rather than of the whole people of the United States. If this was the case, then states ought to be able to "nullify" unconstitutional acts of Congress. Acting under this theory, the two leading Republicans, Thomas Jefferson and James Madison, drew up resolutions that were introduced into the Kentucky and Virginia legislatures. The Kentucky and Virginia resolutions were not identical, but they made the same point. This was that under the Constitution the people had delegated only certain powers to the national government that were clearly spelled out. Any other powers were left to the states.

According to Jefferson and Madison in the Virginia and Kentucky resolutions, the national government had overstepped its powers when it passed the Alien and Sedition Acts, and they asked other states to back them up. None of the other states did, however. But the idea that the states could "nullify" laws passed by the national government was used later by the Southern states in trying to uphold "states' rights" against the national government.

In any case, there was a good deal of opposition to the Alien and Sedition Acts. The laws were allowed to die when the new president came in after the next election, and the people convicted under them were pardoned. Today, the Alien and Sedition Acts are famous among students of American government, for they stand as a warning, a shining lighthouse telling government where it should not sail. In the end, they had a good effect, although that may not have been the opinion of Matthew Lyon and the others put in jail under them. Once again, we can see how this first government set the United States on a course that would continue for a long time.

CHAPTER VIII

The Revolution of 1800

The reason why the new president was so quick to pardon those convicted under the Alien and Sedition Acts was quite simple: The new president was Thomas Jefferson, the leader of the Republicans.

He almost didn't make it. The election of 1800 was important for several reasons. For one, it showed that the Founding Fathers had not done a perfect job when they wrote the Constitution: Changes had to be made in the system for choosing a president. More important, it made it clear that the new government could survive a shift in powers. This shift is one of the great stumbling blocks in establishing new democracies. Often enough they get off to a good start under the first government. But when the officeholders are voted out in favor of new ones, frequently the old officers refuse to leave, get the army behind them (the generals are usually of their party), and take over as dictators. But the election of 1800 led to an easy transition of power, and in the United States, governments ever since have followed this precedent. Never have we had a president who tried to stay in office when his term was up.

The main candidates for president in the 1800 elections were the incumbent—a Federalist, John Adams—and the leader of the Republicans, Thomas Jefferson. There were other candidates, but Adams and Jefferson were the primary ones. The Federalists were certain they had done a good job and ought to be returned to office. They had, so they believed, built a strong system that would lead to a prosperous nation. They were horrified to think that the Republicans might shut down the Bank of the United States, might involve the nation in some alliance with France that would ruin trade with England, and might damage the credit of the new country, which Hamilton's policies had restored. There was some reason for their fears: Jefferson had made it clear that he hated commerce and the cities it grew in: Might he not work against the merchants and shippers the Federalists believed the country's prosperity depended on?

But the majority of Americans had turned against the Federalists. They had come to think that Adams, Hamilton, and their supporters were an elitist group who wanted the wealthy and better educated to lead and the rest to follow. The Alien and Sedition Acts in particular had given rise to fears that the Federalists might be trying to set themselves up as dictators.

The Republicans, on the other hand, at least appeared to be firmly against dominance by the wealthy and wellborn. As we have seen, Jefferson believed that the heart of a democracy lay in people who grew their own food, built their own houses and barns, made their own clothing—the independent farm families who were the typical Americans. They voted heavily for the Republicans.

The election campaign of 1800 was an intensely bitter one. Federalists claimed that Jefferson was an atheist who would turn the nation over to the French; that he had no morals, didn't believe in marriage, had illegitimate children—and other lies even far worse. Republicans said that Adams was a mere lackey of the British, that he would turn the government over to Hamilton and would set up a monarchy worse than that

In 1800, the nation turned against the Federalists, led by Washington, Hamilton, and Adams, who many Americans thought were too elitist, in favor of the Republicans, led by Jefferson and Madison. Historians tend to agree that the Federalists probably had outworn their welcome. Nonetheless, they had put the United States on a sound footing and opened the way for the development of industry. One of the early industrialists who benefited was Samuel Slater. In 1789, he came to America as a young man, precisely as the nation was getting started. Slater built a textile empire, the first in a long line of American industrial complexes.

of George III, against whom Americans had fought the Revolution. It would seem impossible that people who expressed such heated hatreds against each other could ever join in a government to work for the general good. (The story of the election of 1800 is told in *The Jeffersonian Republicans* in this series.)

The Federalists were shocked, indeed stunned, by their defeat. Their struggle against the Republican faction of Jefferson, Madison, and their allies had been long and bitter. They could not understand what had gone wrong, and they did not retire from office happily, but went snarling and

Slater had worked as an apprentice in a cotton-spinning mill in England. It was illegal to export plans of factory machinery from England. Slater had all the plans in his head and designed the first spinning mill in America. This is a drawing of such a mill, showing the machines at work. Actually, there would have been many more workers at the machines.

snapping. But they went: However distraught they were by seeing Jefferson in the presidency, they did not even consider trying to hold onto power by force.

They were right to let the constitutional system take its course. Jefferson, in his first Inaugural Address, sought to bring Americans back together again. "Let us, then, fellow citizens, unite with one heart and one mind," he said. "We are all Republicans, we are all Federalists."

Historians usually see the Federalist Era as a struggle between the Federalists, led by Washington and Hamilton, and the Republicans, led by Jefferson and Madison. With the election of Jefferson, the Republicans clearly had won, especially since he was succeeded by his friend James Madison. In general, historians tend to side with the Republicans, whom they see as having been substantially more democratic than the Federalists.

But we need to be careful about categorizing all Federalists as well-born and wealthy. Alexander Hamilton was raised as a poor boy (although he was the son of a man fallen from the British aristocracy) and built his success on talent, ambition, and drive—exactly the sort of story we most appreciate in a land where it is supposed that anybody can rise. Other important Federalists were also self-made, such as Robert Morris, who had found money for Washington to fight the Revolution.

A second point to keep in mind is that the Federalists, elitist or not, did a great deal that was right for America in

Not all the Federalists were born into wealthy families. Robert Morris came to the United States as a youth with little money, and he received little education here. But he rose to become one of the richest people in the United States, before over speculation in land ruined him.

their twelve years in office. In particular, they dealt coolly with the threat of war with both England and France in turn, and they set the United States on the road to becoming the most successful commercial and industrial nation in human history. Many people would insist that the favoritism Hamilton and the Federalists showed toward trade—business, in today's terms—has given us a nation that is too much concerned about money and possessions, at the expense of more humanitarian values, like concern for other humans, help for the needy, care for children, protection for the environment. In Jefferson's philosophy these ideals ranked higher than the drive for profit. But it cannot be denied that the Federalists accomplished much in getting the United States off on the right foot—they were the right people at the right time, many historians will say.

But their time had ended. By 1800, Americans had come to feel that they did not need a small elite group, however experienced and politically wise, to guide them. They wanted their voices to be heard, and in choosing Jefferson and the Republicans, they got a government that intended to listen.

CHAPTER IX

A Coda: Marbury v. Madison

Jefferson's hopes for complete political reconciliation were in vain, of course. We all know that the factions of the 1790s were only a pale foreshadowing of the modern political parties that we know today. Even as Jefferson spoke his Inaugural Address, a new Federalist leader was about to carry the banner to a new field of battle. The story of how John Marshall, appointed by Adams in the last hours of his presidency to be chief justice of the Supreme Court, solved the problem of unconstitutional acts of Congress is a complex one. It reaches back to the Constitutional Convention of 1787 and is summed up in the phrases "separation of powers" and "checks and balances." Separation of powers means that the president, the Congress, and the Supreme Court each have their own powers and duties. That is, the Supreme Court does not write laws, the president does not try cases, the Congress does not appoint cabinet members and other federal officers. Checks and balances means that these three branches prevent one another from having too much power, or indeed from taking over the government altogether.

This idea of separating the U.S. government into three branches that would check and balance one another was not uppermost in the minds

John Marshall is considered by most historians to be the most important of all Supreme Court justices. His opinions in one significant case after another were critical in shaping how the Supreme Court acts.

of the delegates to the Constitutional Convention when they first gathered in Philadelphia in May of 1787. But as the debates progressed, separation of powers came to be talked about more and more, until by the end most of the delegates were convinced that the checks and balances system ought to be deeply embedded in the new government. Indeed, they came to believe so thoroughly in checks and balances that occasionally they intentionally violated the principle of separation of powers to make the checks work. So, for example, they gave the president the right to veto laws passed by the Congress—letting the executive in on the legislative process. But in order to keep the president from having the final word, they allowed Congress to override the president's vetoes by a two-thirds majority. Similarly, they allowed the president to appoint whomever he wanted to various posts to help him govern, like the secretary of state or the attorney general, but only with the approval of the

Senate—giving a legislative body some say in executive matters. And so it went, round and round, each power in one branch balanced by a power in another branch, sometimes overlapping one another.

But, in fact, the delegates to the Constitutional Convention did not quite finish the job. They provided for a Supreme Court, which they believed would have a check on the other branches, but they never really spelled out completely what the Court could and could not do. In particular, they did not say whether it had a right to decide whether laws passed by the state legislatures or the Congress conflicted with the Constitution.

This was a serious omission. Suppose, for example, that the Congress passed a law putting off elections for several years, so that the people in government could stay in power. Suppose the president signed this law. Such a law would clearly be contrary to the Constitution, which says how often elections for various offices must be held. Who would have the power to strike down such an unconstitutional law? Or as we put it today, who was to interpret the Constitution?

The framers of the Constitution had various ideas. Some thought that the House of Representatives should have this power, others thought the Senate should; still others thought both together should; and others thought the state governments should be allowed to strike down unconstitutional acts. In truth, the whole problem was never carefully thought through.

It had to be settled. As soon as the new government was in place, Congress passed the Judiciary Act of 1789. This was a rather long, complicated piece of legislation, but it did two main jobs. First, it set up a system of federal courts to deal with issues that the state courts could not really handle—say, lawsuits involving ships going from state to state. Second, the new Judiciary Act said specifically that the Supreme Court could throw out *state* laws that it felt conflicted with the Constitution. The Founding Fathers had clearly meant the federal government to have this power, but they had not explained exactly how it was to be done. Now the Judiciary Act spelled it out, and over two hundred years later, that part of the act is still in force.

We must understand that the Judiciary Act of 1789 does not allow the Supreme Court to look over laws passed by the states and say which ones are constitutional and which ones are not. It can make such a judgment only when the right kind of case is brought before it. Let us suppose that the State of New York passed a law levying duties on eggs coming into New York from Connecticut and New Jersey. Such interstate duties are forbidden under the Constitution. A Connecticut poultry farmer who refused to pay the duty would be arrested in New York and found guilty. He would appeal his sentence to the federal courts on grounds that the New York law violated the U.S. Constitution. It would be up to the U.S. Supreme Court to decide if the farmer was right and, if so, to strike down the law as unconstitutional. But the Court could not consider the matter at all until such a case came before it. We call such action of the Court *judicial review*, and, like the cabinet, it has become a major element of our national government without being specified in the Constitution.

The Judiciary Act of 1789 is obviously a very important piece of legislation. But it still left undecided how *federal* laws that conflicted with the Constitution would be struck down. As it turned out, the Supreme Court would decide that for itself. At the time, many people were well aware that this question had to be settled. We can see now that the Supreme Court, especially its third chief justice, John Marshall, was waiting for the right opportunity to assert judicial review of acts of Congress.

The opportunity did not come until 1803, when the Supreme Court was asked to review what is now one of the most famous cases ever in the United States, *Marbury v. Madison*. Ironically, the case was not a terribly important one. A man named James Marbury (along with others) had been appointed a justice of the peace in Washington by President John Adams a few hours before Adams's term as president expired.

The Supreme Court has the power to overthrow state laws that it considers unconstitutional. In 1954, it struck down laws requiring the racial segregation of schools, in the famous case Brown v. Board of Education.

However, there had not been time enough for the actual appointment papers to be delivered to Marbury before Adams left office. The new president, Thomas Jefferson, decided not to honor Marbury's appointment, so Marbury sued.

The case of *Marbury* v. *Madison* is tricky. Marbury's lawyer claimed that under the Judiciary Act of 1789, Marbury was entitled to get his appointment as justice of the peace. Chief Justice John Marshall, however, ruled that the section of the Judiciary Act giving the Court authority to hear the case went against a certain clause in the Constitution.

The Supreme Court also has the power to strike down national laws passed by Congress that the Court believes to be unconstitutional. In 1986, hundreds lined up outside the Supreme Court building to hear the justices' opinion on the Gramm-Rudman law, which required the federal government to balance its budget. The Court ruled the law unconstitutional.

Marbury might well be entitled to his appointment, Marshall suggested; but no matter what the Judiciary Act said, the Constitution did not give the Supreme Court authority to rule in this kind of case. Congress, in other words, had tried to change the Constitution, which it had no right to do.

Marbury v. *Madison* was the first time—and the last until 1857—that the Supreme Court declared a law passed by Congress to be unconstitutional. The Supreme Court—Chief Justice John Marshall, really—had decided, along with many other Americans who had thought about this problem, that it had this power. Startlingly, nobody made much of a fuss about the Court's ruling: Many people concerned with the problem thought that somebody had to make such judgments, and it might best be the Supreme Court.

Many historians today believe that John Marshall's logic in *Marbury* v. *Madison* was not always on target. Some legal experts think that the Supreme Court should not have so much power, and it is certainly true that the Supreme Court today rules on all sorts of issues that would have shocked the Founding Fathers.

But it is difficult to see how anything else would have worked. If a case comes to the Supreme Court involving a law that appears to be unconstitutional, the Court really has no choice but to decide one way or another. And if it decides that the law is unconstitutional, lawyers, government officials, and private citizens will realize that nobody need obey the law, and it will become ineffective. In any case, however shaky Marshall's reasoning was in *Marbury* v. *Madison*, the case established the power of the Supreme Court to strike down any laws it deems unconstitutional. It is true that the people could decide to amend the Constitution to take this power away from the Supreme Court. But what would be put in its place?

The Supreme Court, in deciding that an act of Congress could not be enforced because it violated the Constitution, was one branch of government proclaiming itself to have the final say about what any clause of the Constitution meant. But, of course, the Court had to rely on the executive branch to carry out judicial decisions; and then, too, Congress can always make rules about how the Court is supposed to act—even to say how many justices there will be. But in 1803, the U.S. Supreme Court had six Federalist justices and no Republicans. In the interparty struggle the Federalists had the last word, because after *Marbury* v. *Madison*, the principle had been established that the U.S. government—or the judicial

The significance of the Federalist period was the creation of certain major institutions in the American political system that were not mentioned in the Constitution, or even envisioned by the men who wrote it. Among those institutions are political parties, the cabinet, and review by the Supreme Court of laws for their constitutionality. In this picture of the Supreme Court as composed in 1988, Chief Justice William Rehnquist is front row, center.

branch of it—would be the final judge of what the different governments, state and national, could and couldn't do. Jefferson's idea of states making those decisions, though proposed again from time to time between the 1830s and 1950s, was never able to replace judicial review as set by John Marshall and his fellow justices in 1803.

Thus the American system of democratic government is founded on the Constitution, the architectural drawing that must be followed carefully in order to keep the building safe and secure. But our government also depends on some extraconstitutional elements that the builders found necessary to install to make the structure function smoothly. Without the cabinet, the party system, and judicial review, in particular, but even without the two-term limit for presidents, executive privilege, and the rejection of a "high-toned" presidency, the U.S. government would be very different—if indeed it would have survived—from what we know today.

BIBLIOGRAPHY

For Students

Bober, Natalie. *Thomas Jefferson: Man on a Mountain*. New York: Atheneum, 1988.

Faber, Doris, and Harold Faber. *The Birth of a Nation: The Early Years of the United States*. New York: Atheneum, 1989.

Meltzer, Milton. *George Washington and the Birth of Our Nation*. New York: Franklin Watts, 1986.

——. *Thomas Jefferson: The Revolutionary Aristocrat*. New York: Franklin Watts, 1991.

O'Brien, Steven. *Alexander Hamilton*. New York: Chelsea House, 1989.

Osborne, Mary Pope. *George Washington: Leader of a New Nation*. New York: Dial, 1991.

For Teachers

Elkins, Stanley, and Eric McKitrick. *The Age of Federalism*. New York: Oxford University Press, 1993.

McDonald, Forrest. *Alexander Hamilton: A Biography*. New York: W.W. Norton, 1979.

Malone, Dumas. *Jefferson and the Ordeal of Liberty*. Vol. 3. Boston: Little, Brown, 1969.

——. *Jefferson and the Rights of Man*. Vol. 2. Boston: Little, Brown: 1951.

Miller, John C. *The Federalist Era: 1789-1801*. New York: Harper, 1960.

Shalope, Robert E. *The Roots of Democracy: American Thought and Culture: 1760-1800*. Twayne's American Thought and Culture Series. Boston: Twayne, 1990.

INDEX

and election of 1800, 72, 73-74, 75, 76
and France, 39, 41, 42, 51, 62, 64
Inaugural Address of, 74, 77
Kentucky and Virginia resolutions of,
   70
library of, **52**
philosophy of, 51-52, 53, 72, 76
and political parties, 45
as president, 71, 73-74
as Republican, 53, 62, 71, 75
as secretary of state, 20, 61
as vice president, 63
judicial branch, *see* Supreme Court
judicial review, 84, 85
Judiciary Act (1789), 79-82

Kentucky Resolution, 70

Lafayette, Marquis de, **38**
land claims:
   of farmers, 32-34
   and foreign policy, 35, 42, 66
   and Indians, 32, **32**, 33
   Louisiana territory, 66
   Northwest Territory, 42
   of Spain, 13-14, 66
leaders, natural, 48
League of Nations, 42
legislative branch, *see* Congress
Louisiana territory, 66
Louis XVI, King of France, beheading of, **40**
Lyon, Matthew, 68, 69, 70

Madison, James, 17
and election of 1796, 61
and election of 1800, 73
Kentucky and Virginia resolutions of, 70
philosophy of, 51, 52, 53
and political parties, 16, 45, 50
as Republican, 53, 75
Marbury, James, 80-82

Marbury v. *Madison,* 80-83
Marshall, John, 77, **78**, 80-83, 84
Mississippi River, 14, 66
money, 22, 25, 27
Morris, Robert, 75, *75*
Mount Vernon, 55, *56*, 57

Neutrality Proclamation, 41-42
New England, commerce in, 11-12
New York, wartime commerce in, 40
Northwest Territory, 42

party system, *see* political parties
Peale, Charles Willson, portraits by,
   50, 51
Pearl Harbor, 42
Philadelphia:
   Constitutional Convention in, 55-56
   election day in, **59**
   Independence Hall in, **10**
   Second Street in, **13**
   Walnut Street jail in, *53*
   wartime commerce in, 40
Pitt, William the Younger, **36**
political parties, 45-54
   campaigns of, **46**
   and differing philosophies, 47, 51,
      53-54, 67
   in England, 15, 54
   as extraconstitutional, 54, 84, 85
   factional fighting of, 56
   Founding Fathers on, 16, 45, 47, 67
   national conventions of, **16**
   and strong central government, 47-50
   Washington on, 15-16, 45, 58-59, 67
   see also Federalists; Republicans
Polk, James K., **46**
president:
   checks and balances on, 78-79, 83
   and Constitution, 9-10
   executive privilege of, 44, 85

JAMES LINCOLN COLLIER is the author of a number of books both for adults and for young people, including the social history *The Rise of Selfishness in America*. He is also noted for his biographies and historical studies in the field of jazz. Together with his brother, Christopher Collier, he has written a series of award-winning historical novels for children widely used in schools, including the Newbery Honor classic, *My Brother Sam Is Dead*. A graduate of Hamilton College, he lives with his wife in New York City.

CHRISTOPHER COLLIER grew up in Fairfield County, Connecticut and attended public schools there. He graduated from Clark University in Worcester, Massachusetts and earned M.A. and Ph.D. degrees at Columbia University in New York City. After service in the Army and teaching in secondary schools for several years, Mr. Collier began teaching college in 1961. He is now Professor of History at the University of Connecticut and Connecticut State Historian. Mr. Collier has published many scholarly and popular books and articles about Connecticut and American history. With his brother, James, he is the author of nine historical novels for young adults, the best known of which is *My Brother Sam Is Dead*. He lives with his wife Bonnie, a librarian, in Orange, Connecticut.